Corvette

This book was devised and produced by Multimedia Publications (UK) Ltd.

Editor: Jeff Groman
Design: Brian Harris
Picture Research: Mirco Decet, Virginia Landry
Production: Arnon Orbach

ISBN 0 8317 1789 0

First published in the United States of America by Gallery Books, an imprint of W.H.Smith Publishers Inc., 112 Madison Avenue, New York, NY 10016.
Originated by D.S. Colour International Ltd, London
Printed by Cayfosa, Barcelona, Spain
Dep. Leg. B-34152-1984

CORVETTE

Front endpaper: *A 1969 Corvette with Mako Shark panels.*
Below: *1980 coupé with optional L-82 engine.*

CORVETTE

Nick Baldwin with Tom Falconer

Left: *In foreground 1967 convertible with 6 liter capacity engine and 4-speed manual gearbox, with extensively customized example in background with larger 7 liter engine.*

Contents

INTRODUCTION

In the early 1950s the US motor industry was booming. Every year the cars got longer, wider and lower. V8 engines, first mass produced by Ford in the 1930s, dominated the luxury markets. Chevrolet didn't have a V8. Chevrolet's image at this time was mom, pop and the kids in a six-cylinder four-door. They were battling for top sales with Ford. If you wanted performance from your General Motors car Cadillac had some great convertibles and two-door coupés.

In Italy, Germany and England, Ferrari, Porsche, Jaguar, Austin Healey and MG made cars with small engines but good power-to-weight ratios. General Motors realized the Chevrolet's image could start costing them a vital market share unless they gained a more glamorous image. The result was a dream car produced for the annual Motorama show.

Chevrolet's dream car was a sporty two seater with a European flavor; it had a cut-away door in the roadster style with no winding windows and headlamps set back behind mesh grilles. When the car first appeared at New York's Waldorf Hotel in January 1953, no convertible top was fitted, but it was put on for the Miami show the following

month. The top folded out of sight under a lifting rear body panel, a feature of every Corvette convertible since.

The public raved about the car. Production began at Flint, Michigan, in June 1953. Three hundred identical cars were produced by the end of the year, all white with a red interior and finished with a two-speed Powerglide automatic gearbox.

The Motorama show car prototype was the brainchild of the head of GM styling, Harley Earl, and Ed Cole, Chevrolet's head of engineering. Cole's enthusiasm for the Corvette remained with him through his career, which culminated with his appointment as president of GM, the world's manufacturing giant.

After the pilot plant at Flint had produced three hundred cars, the assembly process was moved to St Louis, Missouri, where more than half a million Corvettes were assembled.

The 1953 Corvette (below left and below) *went from concept to production in only eighteen months, without the benefit of market research or conventional development. The awkward shaped top and detachable side screens were leaky and unpopular, but the car was amazingly modern by the standards of the time and boosted Chevrolet's tired image.*

Bottom: *1954 was the first full year of mass production for the new Corvette. The cars could not be sold as fast as they were built. A variety of colours were offered to try and move the cars which, for the first 300, had all been Polo White.*

DREAM DESIGNS... FABULOUS CARS

Since the early days of the Motorama shows General Motors have become expert at unveiling a dream, experimental or racing car in the full knowledge that they are going to produce something remarkably like it in the not too distant future. It pre-sells the concept and conditions the mind of the market without jeopardizing sales of existing cars. More than 30 Corvette dream and experimental cars have been shown in finished form to the public and many more have been built as full-size non-running models. Some chassis have been rebodied as many as three times to make three different show cars.

The Sting Ray racer is significant in that it accurately

portrayed the shape of the 1963 Corvette in 1959. Built on a spare Corvette SS chassis from 1957, it had never raced for Chevrolet because of a joint agreement between the big manufacturers not to compete with works teams. To get round this ruling the Sting Ray was financed by GM's new chief of staff and styling, Bill Mitchell, who directly influenced every Corvette until 1982. Mitchell is said to have bought the racing chassis for one dollar. He had it rebodied in his corporate studio as the Sting Ray with a fluid new form that owed nothing to any previous car from either side of the Atlantic. When developed for production for the years 1963-7 it would become for many people the most beautiful sports car ever built.

The shape distinctly divides the upper and lower halves of the car, hiding the tops of the wheels and then emphasizing them with streamlined bulges on the upper

Below left: Shown by GM at the launch of the 1978 Corvettes at Milford proving ground, the 1957 red SR 2 racer with two other racing styling exercises.

Below: *Introduced in 1953, the Corvette was not originally aimed at a youth market as this contemporary GM photograph shows. Based on the Motorama show car, only 300 were built, all finished in Polo White with red interior.*

Bottom: *In the background, the Sting Ray competition car S, first seen in 1959. It makes an interesting comparison with Styling's full-size mockups for the 1963 models.*

side. The racer had fully tilting front and rear ends and a 'D-type' fairing behind the driver's head. Bill Mitchell financed all its racing career himself culminating in the SCCA National Championship in its class for Dick Thompson in 1960. The car was re-adopted by General Motors for 1961 as a show car and then returned to Mitchell's private collection.

The Shark

Mitchell then produced another show car for the 1962 season. Built on a standard 1961 Corvette chassis, the Shark dream car was a pastiche of the new car whose design was already fixed. It lacked the proportions of either the Sting Ray racer or the new 98 inch wheelbase car because it was based on the existing 102 inch chassis. However, it did have a supercharged engine, flip-up rear turn indicator and brake lamps, side exhausts with exposed headers and a bubble canopy with a periscope rearview mirror. Like the new car it had air conditioning, power steering and power brakes.

The 1963 models, when they were announced, had one big surprise in store – a genuine coupé body with its fast back sweeping to a point and a dramatic divided back window. This feature was used on the Mako Shark II which appeared on the show circuit in 1965 to pre-sell the revolutionary 1968 model. The fast back was louvered and the car had a fully tilting front, something which wouldn't be seen on a Corvette until 1984, though the concealed covers over the wipers did make production for 1968.

Apart from the white Astro Vette roadster and red Aero Coupé show cars, both modified production models, Mako Shark II was the last of the Corvette front engined coupés. The Mako Shark II was modified into the Manta Ray show car, having paced the 1969 Monaco Grand Prix, and now resides with the Mako Shark I at the Alfred P. Sloan Museum at Flint, Michigan.

The switch to mid-engines

The dream cars of the 1970s were all mid-engined for the very good reason that Chevrolet genuinely wanted to go mid-engined with its Corvette. But three factors meant that the '68 Corvette would continue with only minor annual changes through to 1982. The decade started with demands for ever tightening crash survival and emission regulations by the federal government. It is harder for a sports car to adapt itself to either of these than for a big family car, and Chevrolet did not want to add to their difficulties by trying to go mid-engined at the same time. After the fuel crisis of 1974 the Capitol's corporate average fuel economy regulation had to be met as well; since the Corvette went on selling happily and just scraping through all these requirements, the corporation was content.

The five Corvette mid-engined prototypes were fabulous cars. As various world manufacturers introduced their own answer to the mid-engined fashion, Ferrari, Maserati, VW-Porsche, Lotus, Lamborghini, Fiat and the rest, so it became obvious that all of them lacked the daily usability of the front engined Corvette that has become its trademark. The disadvantages of the mid-engine layout, the restricted luggage space, engine access and rearward visibility, were all conveniently avoided. So the 1984 model has a front engine allowing something which has become a Corvette trademark, a really long bonnet.

Compare this 1963 car (below left) *with the Sting Ray racer.*
The Sting Ray racing car (below) *was campaigned by Bill Mitchell as a private entry to circumvent the manufacturers' agreement among themselves not to have works cars.*
The Shark (bottom), *later renamed the Mako Shark I, was a 1961 model.*

Some show cars were directly derived from production cars. Appearing at car shows in late 1963, this convertible (right inset) *had outside exhausts as favored by styling chief Bill Mitchell, which finally made production in 1965.*

The dream car and the production car derived from it. Bill Mitchell (far right inset) *stands between the Mako Shark II and the 1968 C 427 coupé.*

Below: *1967 customized convertible with 7 liter engine.*

GOODYEAR
POLYGLAS - G70-15

Far left: *The impressive Mako Shark II.*

The Manta Ray (bottom) *was a restyled version of the Mako Shark II, and in its final form was seen at the 1969 Monaco Grand Prix ceremonials.*

Indianapolis Pace Car Replica (left). *The light silver bottom half and dark top half theme of the Mako Sharks I and II finally saw production in this limited edition in 1978.*

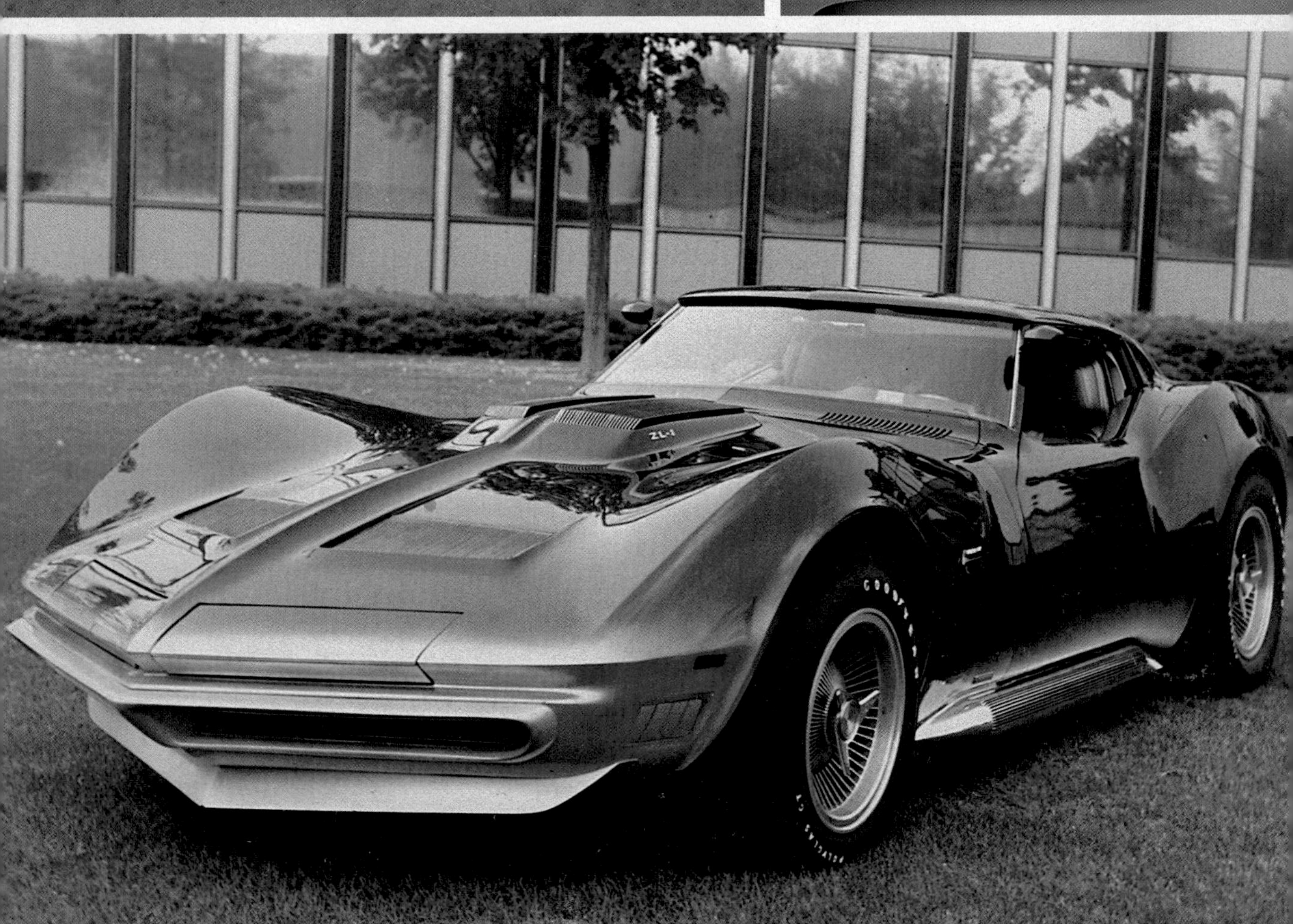

Popularly known as the Moby Dick, this Astro-Vette (far left) *was based on a production 1968 roadster.*

Below left: *A 1968 Corvette coupé. The dream car as suggested by the Mako Shark II was enormously popular with the public and finally sold more than half a million cars of this outstanding shape.*

Below: *1982 Corvettes stockpiled prior to delivery at the new Bowling Green, Kentucky, plant. This facility of more than one million square feet represents an enormous investment in a fiber glass sportscar production line.*

Bottom: *Corvette production line.*

Overleaf: *1980 Corvette.*

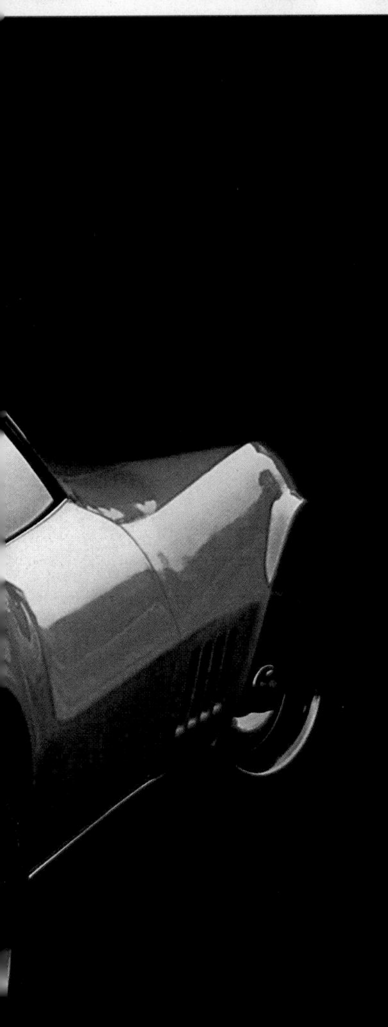

٥٨٣٦٥٠
S.A.
PRIV.
583650

GOODYEAR
EAGLE GT

A DECADE OF DECISION

The new V8 overhead valve engine gave the 1955 Corvette so equipped just the performance which was needed. Though never advertised, a limited number of three-speed V8 1955 models were made, but since the public was not made aware of them they did nothing for the Corvette's performance image.

The year 1955 had also seen the introduction of the two-seater Ford Thunderbird and this undoubtedly gave GM management sufficient confidence in their concept to see if a success could be made of it. The Thunderbird came with a V8, options of manual or automatic transmission, power steering, power brakes, electric windows and plastic detachable hard-top. Though the Corvette was shorter, wider and lower, in 1955 the T-Bird definitely looked the better car.

In 1956 suddenly everything came right for the Corvette.

The T-Bird had served its purpose, going on to gain extra seats and to become fat, and the Corvette began its inevitable progression towards being the biggest selling sports car of all time. The slab sides of the earlier car were given a new sculptured cove extending back into the doors, which now had winding windows with the option of electric operation and external handles. An elegant detachable hard-top was available as a $200 option and the convertible top could be power operated.

Best of all the base engine was boosted from 195 to 210 bhp with optional 225 and 240 bhp engines. The standard transmission was a three-speed manual with Powerglide two-speed automatic $175 extra. If the optional 3.27:1 rear axle was specified, this car would do 100 mph in second gear. The 240 bhp engine used two four-barrel carburetors on top of an aluminum manifold giving the car a top speed of 130 mph. This performance was not really within the capability of the car's brakes, suspension or tires, though the same criticism also applied to other 1950s cars of similar performance.

For 1957 fuel injection was introduced that, when combined with the optional cold air induction system, raised the power to 283 bhp and four-speed transmission was now available. A limited slip differential helped spread

Below: *1956 marked a simple but clever restyling of the old car, losing the faired headlamps and rearlight pods and gaining an elegant sculptured cove available in contrasting body colors. A detachable hard top was offered as an alternative to the convertible top, or both could be had at extra cost. The 1957 car looked identical, but offered fuel injection and four speed transmission.*

this vast amount of power between the skinny back tires. Better brakes came too if you ordered the regular production option 684, which also included heavy duty racing suspension. The special brake linings were Ceremetalix but were tricky for street use in that they required to be warm before they worked evenly.

A 1957 Corvette with fuel injection is to most enthusiasts the most desirable of all the first ten years of Corvettes, combining staggering performance and a pure and simple body with just one headlamp per side at the front, and nothing but bumpers for adornment.

For 1958 Corvette was pulled into line with the rest of the Chevrolet range. Just as the delightful '57 saloon became the four-headlamped and gross 1958, so the new Corvette collected four headlamps and hefty bumpers. A washboard was added to the bonnet, fake air outlets to the coves and two immense ridges to the trunk lid. Ducts on either side of the grille were closed but could be used for cooling the front brakes.

One tremendous improvement was the instrumentation, possibly the nicest ever fitted to a Corvette. All the instruments were grouped in a superb cluster with the tachometer as the centerpiece and the speedometer in a concentric arc outside. Fuel temperature, ammeter and oil

pressure gauges flanked these, while the radio, heater controls and clock were properly shared with the passenger. The chassis remained the same as before while a 290 bhp engine was now available.

Whether or not purists liked the more aggressive styling of the 1958, sales were up from 6339 for the '57 to more than 9000 for the '58. For 1959 the hood and trunk lid were cleaned up and it became possible to get Delco Moraine sintered metallic brake linings as a separate option at just $26.90 rather than buying a full racing package to improve the brakes. For 1960 a virtually unchanged car from the 1959 pushed production over the 10,000 mark. For the last two years of the wrap-around windscreen Corvette, a new tail was introduced which looked much like the Sting Ray which was to follow. With a total of four tail lights this much smoother rear end still included a trunk, 1962 being the last year for this feature. The front end was cleaned up as well, mesh replaced the grille teeth and the headlight bezels were toned down by painting them body color.

The year 1962 was to be distinguished by the lack of chrome trim around the body curve while the engine size was increased from 283 to 327 cubic inches, equivalent to 5.4 liters. The most powerful engine was now a 360 bhp fuel injection engine.

1958 was the year that the big Chevrolet passenger cars went to four headlamps and the Corvette had to follow suit (below left).

This 1958 version (below) *has been fitted with extra wide wheels and tires. Handling of these models is bad at any time and these wide wheels do not improve it.*

Bottom: *Rear view of 1958 model.*

The 1959 Corvette (below) *was simplified by the omission of the washboard in the hood and the trunk strips. Five white-walled tires were a $31 option.*

The rear view of the 1958 model (far right) *shows the twin trunk strips exclusive to that year. Exhaust outlets were hidden within the bumpers, leading to a corrosion problem with these expensive items, but they looked great!* Right: *A detail of the 1958 Corvette – although with a non-standard wheel.*

Corvette
WG-2319

1961 was the first year that the exhaust discharged underneath the car, and behind the wheel. Inset: *The 1961 Corvette had a new tail which anticipated the 1963 shape. The hard top continued as before.*

Left: *It has long been popular to fit aluminum wheels to early Corvettes, but a resurgence of interest in restored cars has now led to these being replaced by the originals.*

There is no limit to what some people will do to a Corvette! This dragster (top) *has a 454 cubic inch V8 as optional on Corvettes from 1970. The drastically dropped nose makes the aerodynamically poor Corvette body more stable at the far end of the quarter mile.*

Center: *The 1961 model.* Above: *The 1962 Corvette.*

FORGING AHEAD 1963-7

The Jaguar E-Type was launched in coupé and convertible form in April 1961 with all independent suspension, disk brakes and 150 mph top speed. Corvette models up to this time had always been broadly comparable to the XK120-150 series, although the latter's disk brakes were far better than the Corvette's drums. The E-Type Jaguar instantly outshone the rest of the world's sports cars and made most of them obsolete overnight. Luckily Chevrolet had not been idle and in 1962 were able to announce the Sting Ray.

Apart from a restyled fuel injection unit the engine and gearbox range continued from 1962 exactly as before. Everything else about the car was brand new. Mitchell's Sting Ray racer shape was all still there but now it was perfect in every detail, a solid sculptural form not just quickly detachable panels on a racing chassis.

The car was built on a four-inch-shorter wheelbase, it was two inches shorter overall and it was also nearly three inches lower. Gone was the wrap-around windscreen first seen on the 1953 Motorama show car. Indeed, of all the world's manufacturers only Auto Union, later Audi, of Germany and the tiny MU Goggomobil continued this theme after General Motors had dropped it.

The windscreen was steeply raked and four headlamps were hidden from view in streamlined housings rotated by twin electric motors operated by a switch on the dash. The rear of the car resembled the 1961-2 but the external luggage compartment was gone, sacrificed to the

demands of a roomier passenger area, a larger fuel tank and revised rear suspension.

State-of-the-art

This new rear suspension represented the latest technology and put Corvette right back up there with the leaders. Ferrari did not get independent suspension on their road cars for a further two years, while Maserati persisted with live axles until the early 1970s. Independent rear suspension and, at last, ball-jointed front suspension gave the 1963 and later Corvettes the ability to go round corners at speeds which would have had the earlier cars switching end. Additionally, a really good power steering system was offered which gave the driver plenty of road feel and, on cars without power steering, there was provision for adjustment to the steering ratio. This choice was extended to the clutch pedal and gearshift lever, both of which also had fast and slow shift positions.

The 1963 coupé has become the great classic of this era mainly because it is distinguished from coupés of the later

The 1963 Sting Ray (below left) *was a radical improvement on previous cars. It had a modern chassis with independent suspension all round.*

The famous split window (below) *was abandoned after only one year of production, because it created a blind spot for the driver just large enough to hide a police motor cycle. It has since become one of the most desirable Corvettes.*

This General Motors publicity shot (bottom) *shows the knock-off aluminum wheels which were not fitted on the production line until the following year, but which many owners bought over the counter. 1963 and 1964 models had non-functional vents behind the front wheel.*

years by its broad dividing strip on the back window. At the time this was universally condemned by the motoring press because it obscured enough of the view through the centrally mounted driving mirror for a police motorcycle to hide undetected. Bill Mitchell had to bow to popular pressure and for 1964 the rear window became one piece. Hundreds of '63 coupé owners rushed to their body shops to have their cars updated, while ten years later kits were available to convert the same cars back to their original specification!

The power race

A high performance engine is only useful as long as brakes are available to control it, and by 1961 virtually all the world's high performance cars except the Corvette were using them and buying them in from Britain. Claiming at the time that these brakes lacked the power for the Corvette, in fact the GM Delco Marine division had been developing their own immense four-piston calipers with ventilated disks for all four wheels for 1965. This was to be the last year for Corvette fuel injection until 1985, but these brakes provided the stopping power for the heavy and powerful Mark IV big block engine which made its debut this year.

Shape of cars to come

The supercar era had begun with John de Lorean's clever decision to boost Pontiac's aging image by putting a 348 bhp 6.5 liter 389 into the Tempest compact and calling the whole package a GTO. Corvette couldn't be left behind

in this power race. While other American manufacturers sometimes got more powerful engines into lighter cars for theoretically better 0-60 times, thanks to its independent rear suspension the Corvette could almost always put its power down more effectively than the opposition on the real life roads away from the drag strip.

For 1966 the big block engine was given a full seven liters at 427 cubic inches and in 1967 triple carburetors. In 1967 less than 10 per cent of cars were ordered with automatic transmission, and most of the big blocks without power steering, something which subsequent owners at least must have regretted.

Top: *Factory aluminum wheel which was not as light as it looked, using a heavy pegged adaptor which in turn bolted on to the hub. Spinners were handed – this is for the left side of the car.*

The 1964 coupé had a one-piece back window (above left). *The doors were generously cut into the roof for easy access. The 1963-7 coupés are the only Corvettes that have been made with permanently fixed roofs* (above).

Left: *A 1964 coupé with standard hubcaps on steel wheels. Air conditioning had been available since 1963 and increased the appeal of the Corvette, particularly in the south-west of the States.*

Top: *A 1965 convertible with aluminum knock-off wheels. The big sloping windshield and low driving position makes the Sting Ray an excellent convertible.*

Above: *Fuel injection was introduced in 1957 and was last seen in 1965 when it was found that more performance was available more cheaply by using the big block family of engines. Fuel injection gives the small block up to 375 bhp and exceptional fuel economy.*

A 1967 big block 427 convertible with factory side exhaust and hard top. Unlike the after-market exhaust so often fitted, the factory item had a well-designed aluminum shield to protect passengers' legs from burns.

The headlamps of the Sting Ray models (above) swivelled on electric motors with an instrument panel warning light to indicate if they were not fully up.

Right: *A 1963 coupé at the scene of the General Motors launch of the 1978 range. 1963 was the only year for the metal decorative grilles in the hood.*

Far right: *A 1967 coupé showing the filler cap cover which had a body-colored insert on this year only. A rare option on these Sting Ray coupés was a 36 gallon fuel tank intended for endurance racing. 1967 was the last year of the Sting Ray spelt as two words – when it came back in 1969 it appeared as Stingray.*

Corvette
STING RAY

LEADING THE PACK 1968-82

The same chassis suspensions and front and rear engine choices were carried through to 1968 but there was a styling tour de force which had even more worldwide impact than the 1963 model. In the great traditions of Harley Earl, it gave American car buyers the opportunity to drive something from the future.

From pointed nose to flipped-up tail it was seven inches longer and nearly two inches lower. Its steeply raked windscreen had its wipers hidden under a vacuum operated flap. To lower the front bonnet line, headlamps were now lifted up by vacuum; the front grilles were no longer the main source of engine-cooling air, which was admitted through slots underneath the front body, the technique that is now widely used throughout the world's

motor industry. The convertible had a tiny top that emphasized the pinched waist styling. The coupé now had detachable roof panels that became known as T-roofs and, through the 1971 model year, a detachable back window with its own storage compartment inside the car.

The new shape of the car now determined that the driver and passenger sat closer together and saw the road over an immense bonnet flanked by the contoured bulges over the front wheels. On the center console, fiber optic sensors reported direct information from the car's principal lamps, advising the driver of bulb failure. American police can't stop you without reasonable cause – knowing that all his lights were working properly gave the Corvette owner a special reassurance.

After 1968 had seen an increase in Corvette wheel size from six to seven inches, in 1969 they were increased again to eight inches; also a headlight washer system was

This 1969 convertible (below left) *has the big block 427 and after-market 'outsider' chromed headers. The Stingray name was reintroduced for this model a year after a one-year lapse.*

Below: *A 1968 coupé with the optional domed hubcaps beloved of GM stylists. This car uses the small block 327 – big block engines had an extra hood bulge. The windshield wipers are concealed under an automatic vacuum flap.*

Bottom: *1970-73 cars share the same square-cut tail with squared-off exhaust outlets. There is no trunk; under that long rear deck is a sixteen gallon gas tank and a small baggage space behind the seats. 1970-72 cars have a honeycomb grille behind the front wheel.*

introduced as standard and the outside door handles improved. The small block V8 was increased to 350 cubic inches and a staggering $3000 optional aluminum big block engine, the ZL1, was offered, giving up to 560 bhp. The best evidence currently available suggests that only two were ever fitted to Corvettes, but 69 were fitted to Camaros.

Since its introduction in 1967 the Camaro was being built in hundreds of thousands every year and, as it appealed to a far wider audience than the Corvette, it was in some way a much more effective image builder. None the less the Camaro was always a four seater and as long as it continued to make profits for them Chevrolet were only too happy to continue building their exclusive and very expensive two seater.

Goodbye to the convertible

Much improved by its 1970 facelift, the Corvette got a new federal front bumper in 1973 and a federal rear bumper to go with it in 1974, both covered in flexible polyurethene moldings matching the body color. Emission requirements, principally the need to run on no-lead petrol, reduced the compression ratios in 1971, saw the end of the 454 in 1974 and the introduction of the power robbing catalytic converter in 1975.

The Corvette had been available only as a convertible for its first ten years, but it now bowed to market pressures – no convertibles were built after 1975, when they accounted for only 4500 cars out of more than 33,500 built.

Just looking at the option tables often gives the impression that there is no Corvette worth having after 1971, but practical experience has shown that this simply isn't true. Any Corvette is good for at least 120 mph and simple changes to the exhaust system alone makes 130 plus a possibility. The 1963-7s had 140 mph capabilities but tend to be unstable over 115 due to an excess aerodynamic lift at the front which makes the steering go light. While a correctly optioned 1968-70 car will achieve 150 mph, it won't feel nearly as good at 100 mph as a 1976 does. Not only does the later car have better road noise

insulation and sound deadening that assists driver concentration, but it also has radial tires with their much better directional stability. While it might be a slower 0-60 it will also be more economical. Cars from the late 1970s are capable of better than 20 miles per US gallon at 70 mph.

Towards the 1980s

For 1978 interior space was increased with the introduction of the big back window. To celebrate 25 years of Corvette production, and the use of the Corvette as the Indianapolis pace car, two special editions were produced both of which are now considered very desirable.

The new 1980 car with a shovel nose and aerodynamic tail was faster and lighter. GM's research into reducing weight for federal bumper systems paid off with the substitution of polyurethene honeycombs and fiberglass supports front and rear. This combined with the weight saving of an aluminum rather than a cast-iron differential saved more than 200 pounds in weight.

Below left: *This 1976 Corvette has been adapted to a four-wheel drive sand-dragger. Assume that only the basic body is now Corvette. The Corvette body is ideal for exposure to seawater – fiberglass is what most boats are made of, too!*

Below: *This 1972 convertible would not contain the golfing equipment of this happy couple with the top stowed. An optional rack was available from dealers to increase carrying capacity.*

Bottom: *A 1974 convertible. This was the first year for body-color bumpers front and rear. Less than 10,000 convertibles produced before production finished in 1975 makes these cars particularly desirable.*

Main picture: *This beautiful 1977 model has had its wheels changed for a set of chromed five-spokes.*

Inset: *1976 saw Corvette production pass 40,000 for the first time and was the last year that the Stingray name was used – in future it was just called a Corvette.*

GT RADIAL
GOODYEAR
GT RADIAL

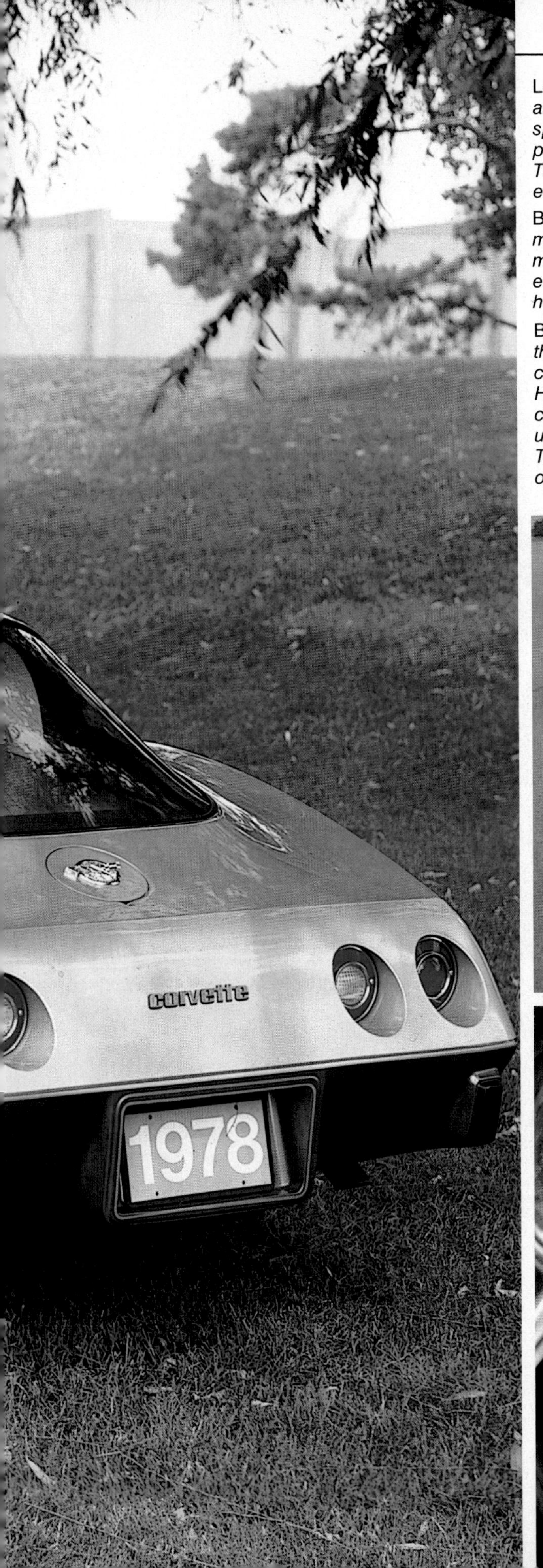

Left: *1978 marked the Corvette's 25th anniversary, which was celebrated with two special editions and a radical increase in passenger room with a big back window. This is the 'silver anniversary' special edition.*

Below: *The new nose and tail of the 1980 model improved streamlining and saved more than 100 lbs in weight. They also emphasized the long nose look which helped make the Corvette so popular.*

Bottom: *First seen in the Pace Car Replica these plastic-framed seats were far more comfortable and gave better side support. Here they are seen fitted into a 1974 convertible body shell, which has been updated with many other later features. These seats were available with real leather or velour inserts.*

CHEVROLET
USA1

Above: *On test on wet roads in England's Lake District, this coupé shows the later egg-crate vent grille and larger side marker lights which distinguished the 1970-72 models.*

Far left and left: *6500 Pace Cars were made as replicas of the actual car which paced the start of the 1978 Indy 500 which was won by Al Unser for Jim Hall's Chaparral team in their first ever entry for this prestigious race. The silver leather interior with special seats was exclusive to the Pace Car, though the seats became standard in 1979.*

1979
POLYSTEEL RADIAL
GOODYEAR

The glass-mirrored roofs first offered on the Pace Car became an increasingly popular option during 1979, as did front and rear spoilers which were offered for the first time. The sports mirrors were still an option, becoming standard the following year.

1982
1982
GOODYEAR
GOODYEAR

Left: *1982 saw the option of a Collectors Edition with special striping, internally and externally, a hatchback rear window and special wheels.*

Below: *For 1980, the aluminum wheel got a new center cab and the 255/60 Eagle radials continued to be a popular optional tire.*

Bottom: *This 1976 coupé has the optional luggage rack mounted well forward and has been converted to right-hand drive for a British enthusiast.*

Corvettes are meant to be driven hard and fast. This 1977 model is fitted with the optional luggage rack, which was a dealer-fitted option.

Left: *1981 was the last year to have a four-speed manual transmission which had been a Corvette option since 1957. It did not return until mid-1984.*

Below: *Chevrolet celebrated the move to the new factory at Bowling Green, Kentucky, with new two-color paint finishes with additional striping. Further fuel economy improvements were achieved with 'cross-fire' fuel injection.*

1984 AND BEYOND

Before production of the 15 year old shape ended in 1982, a further 100,000 cars had been produced, making the total since 1968 in excess of half a million. In 1968 the Corvette was one of the few world sports grand touring cars to combine real performance with the comforts of air conditioning, electric windows, power steering and stereo radio. The availability of these items compensated for the slightly less than impeccable road manners, and anyway the Corvette was always cheaper than the competition.

During the intervening period the rest of the world caught up. Even Lotuses and Jaguars now had air conditioning even if they did use American hardware to achieve it.

The new-look '84

In introducing their new model, Chevrolet decided to meet the competition head-on with a car that made no concessions to anyone and would not be built down to a price. The car was once again entirely new including the first chassis change for 20 years. While the engine was, like the 1982, a small block 350 with 'crossfire' injectors, these latter were now incorporated into a fully styled housing; the multiple engine accessory drive belts were all driven by a single toothed belt.

The chassis is uncompromisingly state-of-the-art. While all previous cars had used steel stampings for most of the

suspension components, the 1984 has forged aluminum front upper and lower wishbones and an all-aluminum five-link rear suspension. The suspension medium both front and rear is horizontal fiberglass transverse springs as seen on the rear of 1982s. The old cast-iron and troublesome brake calipers have been replaced by a lightweight aluminum design made for the car by Girlock in Australia. Wheels are 16 inch with turbo-fan vanes to assist with the removal of heat and, unfortunately, brake dust from the brakes. They carry P255/50VR 16 Goodyear Unidirectional Gatorback tires.

Corvette's chief engineer, Dave McLellan, established that the new Corvette had to equal or beat the Porsche 928s and the Ferrari 308 GTB. Fitted with the optional Z-51 suspension on a closed circuit, it was faster on a slalom course and made the curves with less roll than either. On the open road this suspension has proved to be excessively harsh and many feel that the standard suspension is not a lot better – for the 1985 model there are major improvements to the standard suspension.

Perhaps too much of the ride is sacrificed to meet the competition, but the handling of the 1984 car is delightful and will flatter any driver who gets behind the wheel. The rack and pinion power steering has the feel, feedback and quick response of a manual steered mid-engined circuit car. For 1985 the engine has been given, for the first time in 20 years, eight individual fuel injectors – this takes the maximum speed to more than 100 mph in excess of the federal 55 mph speed limit!

Whatever technicalities might lie underneath, Corvettes still sell primarily for their appearance, and the new model is no exception to the tradition already established by Chevrolet. While keeping a family resemblance to the

Below: *The 1984 Corvette is shorter, lower and wider than its predecessor. Reversing lights are incorporated in the rear quarters to make night-time backing easier and, like every Corvette since 1958, it has grille vents behind the front wheels.*

Camaro, the front and rear still relate to the older models.

The new car is superb from any angle and makes the 928 look old fashioned. The steeply raked screen and the larger rear window, now a genuine hatchback, have reduced the size of the roof panels so that they can now be removed and stowed inside the car in one piece. For the driver, who has the option of an electrically adjustable seat, all instrumentation is digital, one of the best systems around.

During 1980 the cars sold in the United States had to have speedometers which stopped at 85 mph as a safety measure. The Corvette neatly circumvented this ruling by having a colored bar graph as its main speedometer which stops at 85 but an additional digital readout beside it which records higher speeds.

With the 1983 Corvette introduced rather late in March 1983, it was decided to call the new models 1984s and run the model for a year and a half, particularly since it met all the 1984 federal requirements.

Crème de la crème

Continuing the theme that the new Corvette was as good as any sports car, Chevrolet decided to build specially modified cars for Europe and Japan, though no righthand drives were built. Besides having different side and rear

lamp configurations, many of these cars out-perform the domestic product because they are tuned to run on leaded petrol without catalytic convertors. These export versions are normally priced to cost the same as the rival Porsche 928.

Now costing more than $25,000 in the US, the Corvette is far more expensive than any other Chevrolet. Some Cadillac dealers now feel that they should be handling this Cadillac-priced sports car, leaving Chevy dealers to their traditional cheap end of the market. Let's hope that the General has the sense to see that it must always be a Chevrolet Corvette.

Below left: *Corvettes have always looked good in white. The dividing band stretches right around the car.*

Below: *Front view shows detachable license plate cover; an increasing number of American states do not now require marque 'tags'. Front openings are in keeping with Corvette tradition, but contain driving lights and parking/turn signals.*

Bottom: *The 1984 Corvette is the first with four tail-lights since 1968. Back-up lights flank the rear license plate.*

Left: *At the GM technical center at Warren, Michigan, the wind tunnel is in constant use to make the cars more frugal on fuel. Here advanced techniques give visual clues to the airflow over the 1984 model.*

Top: *The 1984 model uses the small block V8 that has been available in every Corvette since 1955. Making extensive use of high-strength lightweight metals in the chassis and suspension, it features for the first time rack and pinion steering.*

Above: *Sixteen-inch wheels with ultra-low-profile uni-directional tires are standard. Driving lights and combined parking and directional signal lights take up the entire 'grille'. Engine-cooling air enters beneath the bumper.*

Above: *Corvette in racing trim designed to challenge the might of Porsche and BMW.*
Back end paper: *1963 Corvette.*

Picture credits

Ed Alexander 22-23, 32-33, 33 top, 35, 36-37, 60-61, 61 top **Chevrolet** 7, 20-21, 25 top right, 26 top, 29 centre, 31 bottom, 44, 58-59, 61 bottom, 62-63, 63 **Tom Falconer** back cover, title page, 8, 9, 11, 12-13 top, 13, 14, 15, 16, 16-17, 17 centre, 17 bottom, 33 bottom, 34-35, 38 bottom, 41, 43, 46-47, 47, 48-49, 50-51, 52-53, 53 bottom **Chris Harvey** 4-5, 12-13 **Bob Hill** cover **Mike Key** 64, back endpaper **Andrew Morland** 23, 24-25 top, 29 top, 42-43 **National Motor Museum** 18-19, 40-41 **The Photo Source** 10, 31 top **Tony Stone Associates** 54-55 **Nicky Wright** front endpaper, 6-7, 17 top, 26-27, 28-29, 29 bottom, 30-31, 38 top, 39, 44-45, 53 top

CORVETTE